The Chinese

THE ANCIENT WORLD

The Chinese

Pamela Odijk

Silver Burdett Press

Acknowledgments

The author and publishers are grateful to the following for permission to reproduce copyright photographs and prints:

ANT: Tony Howard cover; Frithfoto p.9; Otto Rogge pp. 11, 12, 35; Silvestris p. 12; Fred Mercay p. 13 top; Pavel German p. 13 bottom; S. Hodgkiss pp. 22 top right, 23, 26; Peter McDonald p. 41; Coo-ee Historical Picture Library pp. 17, 18; Ronald Sheridan/The Ancient Art and Architecture Collection pp. 15, 19, 20, 24, 25, 27, 28, 29, 31, 32, 34, 37, 38, 41; Werner Forman Archive pp. 21, 22 left bottom, 33, 36.

While every care has been taken to trace and acknowledge copyright, the publishers tender their apologies for any accidental infringement where copyright has proved untraceable. They would be pleased to come to a suitable arrangement with the rightful owner in each case.

First published 1989 by
THE MACMILLAN COMPANY OF AUSTRALIA PTY LTD
107 Moray Street, South Melbourne 3205
6 Clarke Street, Crows Nest 2065

Adapted and first published in the United States in 1991
by Silver Burdett Press, Englewood Cliffs, N.J.

Library of Congress Cataloging-in-Publication Data

Odijk, Pamela
     The Chinese / Pamela Odijk.
        p.   cm. —(The Ancient world)
     Includes index.
     Summary: Discusses the civilization of ancient China,
including its daily life, religion, government, legends, clothing,
food, art, music, and recreation.
     1. China—Civilization—To 1912—Juvenile literature.
[1. China—Civilization—To 1912]   I. Title.   II. Series: Odijk,
Pamela, 1942–
Ancient world
DS721.035   1991
951—dc20   91-10578
     ISBN 0-382-09894-3 (lib. bdg.)   CIP
     ISBN 0-382-24271-8 (pbk.)   AC
Printed in Hong Kong

The Chinese

Contents

The Chinese: Timeline   6
The Chinese: Introduction   9
The Importance of Landforms and
    Climate   11
Natural Plants, Animals, and Birds   12
Crops, Fishing, and Hunting   14
How Families Lived   16
Food and Medicine   19
Clothes   21
Religion and Rituals of the Chinese   23
Obeying the Law   26
Writing It Down: Recording Things   27
Chinese Legends and Literature   29
Art and Architecture   32
Going Places: Transportation, Exploration, and
    Communication   34
Music, Dancing, and Recreation   35
Wars and Battles   37
Chinese Inventions and Special Skills   39
Why the Civilization Declined   41
Glossary   42
The Chinese: Some Famous People and
    Places   44
Index   46

The Chinese: Timeline

Fossil remains of Peking Man (*Homo erectus*) dating from 500,000–100,000 years ago have been found in northern China. These early humans were later replaced by modern humans (*Homo sapiens*) who migrated from elsewhere in Asia.

New Stone Age. Earliest agriculture in China. Pigs, dogs, oxen, chickens, and other animals domesticated; crops such as millet, rice, and vegetables were planted. The first main area of agriculture and urbanization was along the Yellow River.

500,000 B.C.	5000	1800

Qin Dynasty. Capital at Chang'an. The Great Wall was built, along with roads, canals, and other public works. Imperial-style government replaces feudalism.

Han Dynasty. Empire greatly expands in size; trade with Roman Empire along Silk Route. Paper invented. **Examination system** promotes efficient bureaucratic government. Confucianism becomes official state ideology. Buddhism introduced from India.

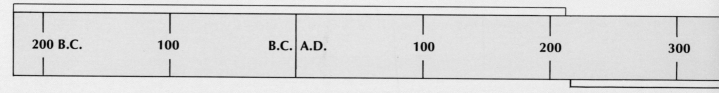

200 B.C.	100	B.C.	A.D.	100	200	300

Period of political disunion. Buddhism becomes popular; art and literature flourish.

Song Dynasty. Capital at Kaifeng until 1127, when north China was conquered by non-Chinese nomads, and at Hangzhou in the south thereafter. Advances in science, technology, and the arts. Overseas trade expands.

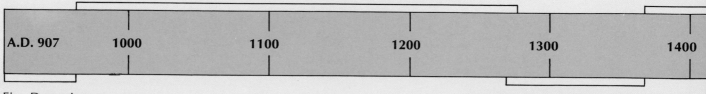

A.D. 907	1000	1100	1200	1300	1400

Five Dynasties Period. Civil war and military rule.

Yuan Dynasty. China conquered and ruled by Mongols, with capital at Beijing. Marco Polo visits China.

Shang Dynasty. Shang kings ruled the Yellow River valley. Land was irrigated. Bronze, silk cloth, and jade used by ruling classes. Chariots, wheat, and goats introduced from western Asia. Earliest surviving Chinese writing dates from this period.

Zhou Dynasty. Zhou kings claim that a **Mandate of Heaven** gives them the right to rule. Government by **feudalism**, with numerous small states ruled by aristocrats loyal to the king. Iron began to be used for tools. Beginning of Chinese literature. Confucius taught ethics and good government; Daoists, Legalists, and others began teaching their beliefs.

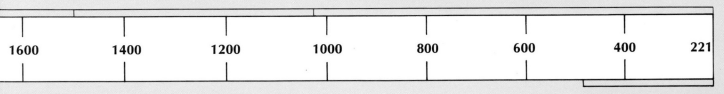

| 1600 | 1400 | 1200 | 1000 | 800 | 600 | 400 | 221 |

Warring States Period: Frequent warfare, with larger states conquering and absorbing smaller ones.

Sui Dynasty. Empire reunified, with capital at Chang'an. Grand Canal built.

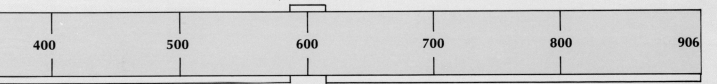

| 400 | 500 | 600 | 700 | 800 | 906 |

Tang Dynasty. Contact and trade with distant lands. Empire is large, powerful, and wealthy; brilliant development of poetry and the arts. High point of Buddhism in China.

Ming Dynasty. Mongols driven out, and Chinese rule restored. China wealthy, powerful, but increasingly isolated from events in the rest of the world.

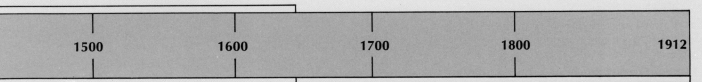

| 1500 | 1600 | 1700 | 1800 | 1912 |

Qing Dynasty. China conquered and ruled by Manchus. Dynasty powerful under first three emperors, but becomes weak during its final century. Increasing Western impact leads to Opium Wars and humiliation by foreign powers. Rebellions and civil wars; revolution and end of dynastic rule.

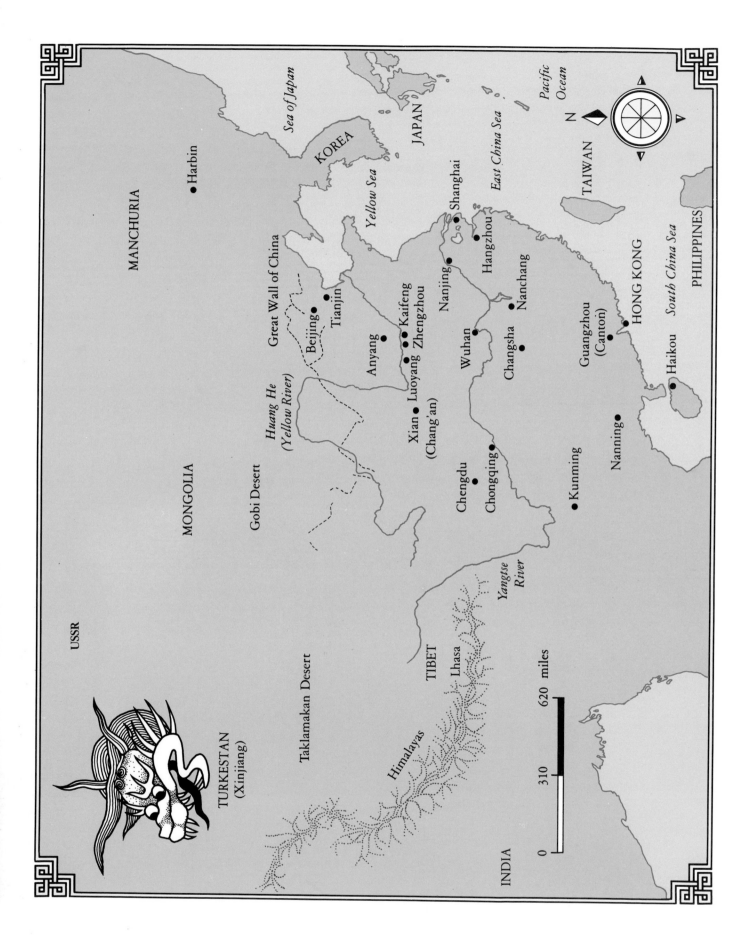

The Chinese: Introduction

Chinese civilization has a history of more than 5,000 years. China developed largely in isolation from the rest of the world. The Chinese called their empire "The Middle Kingdom," and claimed that their emperor ruled "All Under Heaven." The name China comes from the Qin **dynasty** of the third century B.C., when China first became a unified empire. The Chinese and Roman empires traded with each other along the **Silk Route**, but neither knew much about the other.

Europeans became more interested in China after Marco Polo wrote about his travels there in the thirteenth century A.D. Eventually, European influence was one of the causes of the downfall of traditional Chinese civilization.

Chinese civilization changed greatly during its 5,000 year history, but there were also many continuities. Ruling families (dynasties) all promoted an agricultural, family-based society and sought to defend the empire against outside threats.

The Great Wall of China was built during the Qin dynasty to protect the northern frontier.

Name of Dynasty	Some Important Things That Happened
Xia Dynasty 1953–1576 B.C.	Beginning of dynastic rule. First cities and earliest use of bronze in China.
Shang Dynasty 1576–1054 B.C.	Shang kings ruled the Yellow River valley and built palaces and cities. Crops grown in irrigated fields. Bronze, jade, and silk used by ruling classes. Chariots, wheat, and goats introduced from western Asia. Earliest Chinese writing.
Zhou Dynasty 1054–221 B.C.	Empire greatly expanded. Zhou kings claim Mandate of Heaven to rule, and establish feudal system of government. Beginnings of Chinese literature; time of Confucius, China's greatest teacher and philosopher. Iron used.
Warring States Period 481–221 B.C.	Civil wars; large states conquer and absorb smaller ones. Daoism, Legalism, and other philosophical theories compete.
Qin Dynasty 221–206 B.C.	Beginning of imperial-style rule; bureaucratic government replaces feudalism. Strong but harsh government and powerful army. Great Wall built, along with roads and canals. Writing system standardized.
Han Dynasty 206 B.C.–A.D. 220	Strong government with Confucianism as official ideology. Trade with Roman Empire along Silk Route. Art, scholarship, and commerce flourish. Paper invented. Buddhism introduced from India. Invasions, rebellions, and civil war mark end of Han period.
Period of Disunion A.D. 220–581	No unified government, but art and literature flourish. Buddhism gains in popularity.
Sui Dynasty A.D. 581–618	Country reunited. Grand Canal built.
Tang Dynasty A.D. 618–906	Empire large, wealthy, and powerful; one of China's greatest dynasties. Extensive foreign trade. Great literature. Printing and gunpowder invented. High point of Buddhism in China.
Five Dynasties Period A.D. 906–960	Fifty years of civil war.
Song Dynasty A.D. 960–1279	Militarily weak but culturally brilliant. Great age of landscape painting. Large-scale overseas trade.
Yuan Dynasty A.D. 1279–1368	Mongols conquer China but have difficulty ruling resentful population. Peking Opera becomes popular. Marco Polo visits China.
Ming Dynasty A.D. 1368–1644	Chinese rule restored. Famous period for porcelain, architecture, and popular literature. China unaware of rising power of Europe.
Qing Dynasty A.D. 1644–1911	Manchus conquer China. Strong at first, but weakened after 1800 by rebellions and European impact.

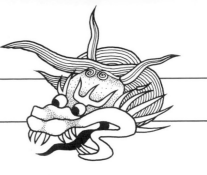

The Importance of Landforms and Climate

China is the third largest country in the world. Its boundaries are formed by the Pacific Ocean in the east, the Amur River in the northeast, two great deserts in the north and northwest, the Himalayas, a mountain system in the southwest, and several ranges of forested mountains in the south. These geographical barriers tended to isolate China from other areas of civilization (India, the Middle East, and Europe) for most of its history.

Two large river systems run through China: the Huang He (Yellow River) in the north and the Yangtse River in central China. Throughout history the great rivers of China have flooded repeatedly, bringing great suffering to the people but also renewing the fertility of the land by depositing silt in the lowlands and **deltas**. This is especially true of the Yellow River, which constantly carries earth from the **loess** hills of the northwest to the North China Plain. North

The Li River near Guilin in southeastern China. These limestone hills were formed by erosion.

China has fertile soil but not enough rain; southern China has ample water but relatively poor soils that require constant fertilization.

Climate

Being so large, China has different climates in different places. The north is relatively dry, with hot summers and cold winters. This part of China is sometimes called the "brown north," because of its dry, wind-blown, but very fertile loess soil.

South China receives abundant rainfall and has a subtropical climate with humid summers and mild winters. Along the southeastern coast, tropical monsoons bring heavy rains each year. This is the "green south," where hills are covered by forests and crops can be grown year-round. Streams provide water for irrigation, and canals are used to transport goods in barges and boats.

Northwestern China (Xinjiang) and Tibet are very dry and largely unsuitable for agriculture.

Natural Plants, Animals, and Birds

Plants

China is home to more than 30,000 species of plants, many of which are unique to China. Dominant vegetation includes temperate forests of both evergreen and deciduous trees, tropical rainforests, grasslands, desert plants, and even mangrove swamps in southern coastal areas. In populated areas, cultivated crops have largely replaced wild plants. Bamboo, found in all but the driest parts of China, is one of the country's most useful plants. It provides the raw material for building, furniture, and tools, and young bamboo shoots are eaten as a vegetable.

China's plant resources vary from region to region. In northern areas, wheat, barley, millet, corn, soybeans, and sorghum are grown, along with cotton, chestnuts, pears, and persimmons. Dates, grapes, and melons are grown in oases in the northwestern deserts. In southern and southeastern areas, rice is the main crop, while tea, mulberry trees, green vegetables, citrus fruits, sugar cane, tobacco, cinnamon, camphor, and bamboo are also cultivated.

Among the most unusual plants native to China are the gingko and dawn redwood trees. These species are so ancient that they are sometimes called living fossils.

Animals and Birds

China's animals include giant and red pandas, lynx, leopards, tigers, wolves, foxes, bears, martens, badgers, weasels, raccoons, and mongooses. Hooved animals include deer, antelope, gazelles, ibex, sheep, goats, yaks, wild boar, oxen and wild horses and camels. In ancient times, rhinoceroses and elephants also were found in China.

China has about one-eighth of the world's bird species, including many hawks, pheasants, parrots, peacocks, and kingfishers. The native Chinese wild chicken is the ancestor of domestic chickens.

China also has about 1,000 species of fish; **carp** are raised in ponds for food. Reptiles include snakes, turtles, and alligators. China is also home to the giant salamander, which measures more than five feet (1.5 meters) in length.

China's wildlife is seriously threatened today by habitat destruction and pollution, and many species have become very rare.

Bamboo grows in many places in China. Giant pandas live in remote bamboo forests in Sichuan Province.

Above: the ibex is one of the many hooved animals that inhabit the desert and mountainous regions of China.

Right: the red panda, which lives in the temperate forests of southwestern China, is an endangered species.

13

Crops, Fishing, and Hunting

Crops

Since the New Stone Age, agriculture has been the basis of the Chinese way of life. **Millet** was grown from the fifth millennium B.C., and rice from the fourth millennium B.C. Wheat was introduced around 1300 B.C. The earliest center of Chinese agriculture was in the loess hills of the upper Yellow River valley.

In ancient times Chinese farmers worked their fields with tools of wood and stone. Iron plows and hoes were invented in the fifth century B.C. Plows were pulled by oxen in the grain fields of the north, and by water buffaloes in the rice **paddy fields** of the south.

The planting and harvesting of crops was done by hand. Ripened stalks of grain were cut with sickles, and sheaves of grain were carried on poles across the shoulders. Grain was threshed by beating it against a wooden frame or pounding it with sticks. The loosened grain was winnowed by tossing it in the air from baskets to let the wind blow away the chaff. In the fourteenth century A.D. a hand-cranked threshing and winnowing machine was invented, making the work of harvesting much easier.

Rice paddy fields must be flooded with water during the growing season, and drained for the harvest. Complex networks of terraces, irrigation channels and dikes were built to control the irrigation of the fields, and sometimes foot-powered pumps were used to bring water to the fields. Fields were fertilized with ashes and manure, and crop rotation was practiced to keep the fields productive year after year.

Chinese farmers grew hundreds of different kinds of vegetables, including cabbage, soy-

Rice paddy fields in southeast China. The Chinese have cultivated rice for the last 6,000 years.

beans and other kinds of beans, peas, and bamboo shoots. Potatoes and sweet potatoes became important crops after they were introduced from South America by the Spanish in the seventeenth century. Fruits included oranges, bananas, litchis, pears, plums, and nuts.

The Chinese also raised many crops to produce fibers for cloth, including mulberry trees (the leaves of which were fed to silkworms), cotton hemp, jute, and **ramie**. Woolen cloth was seldom used except in the far north.

Many domestic animals were kept for farmwork and transportation. Donkeys, mules, and horses were common in the north, while water buffaloes were used more in the south. In the dry north, roads made horse- or ox-drawn wagons, wheelbarrows, and carts practical; in desert areas, camel caravans were used. In the watery south, heavy goods were carried in boats and barges on rivers and canals, while smaller loads were carried on shoulder poles by people walking on narrow paths.

Other domestic animals were raised for food, including pigs, chickens, and ducks. In dry northern areas, sheep, goats and cattle were grazed on the grasslands.

Fishing and Hunting

Fish, caught on lines or in nets in rivers, lakes, and coastal waters, were an important part of the Chinese diet. From as early as 100 B.C., carp were raised in artificial ponds.

Hunting also contributed to the Chinese diet. Small animals and birds were caught and sold as food in town markets. Larger animals were hunted for sport by members of the upper classes in special parks and hunting preserves.

Hunting was considered a sport by the nobility, as shown in this seventeenth century hunting scene.

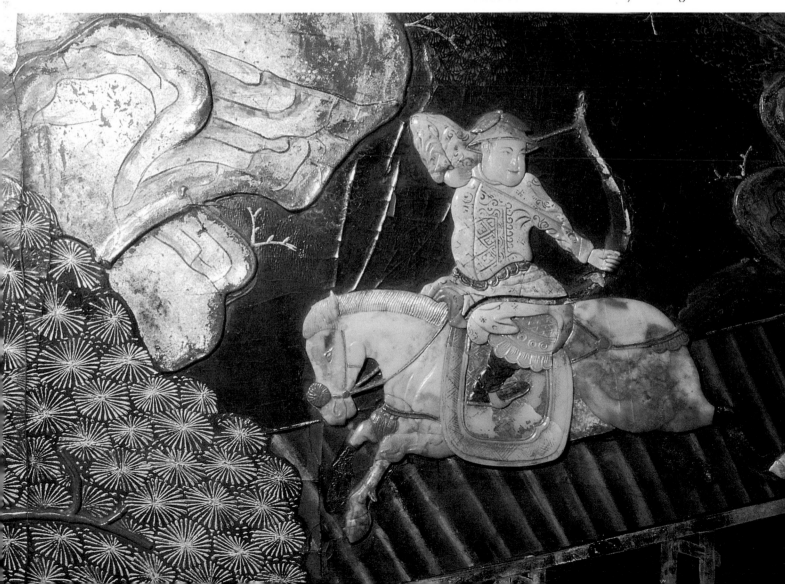

How Families Lived

Villages, Towns, and Cities

Throughout history, most Chinese people have been farmers, and they lived in small villages amidst the fields. Villages in northern China were often located at a crossroads, and were small, compact collections of mud-brick houses. In southern China, villages were often along and narrow, with brick houses strung out along the banks of a river or canal.

Every county in China was centered on a large, walled town, where the local **magistrate** had his **yamen** (offices and official residence). Such towns would also have temples, shops, and a marketplace where farmers from the surrounding countryside could buy and sell things.

Since ancient times, China also contained many large cities, which served as provincial capitals or the capital of the entire nation. Such cities were surrounded by strong walls, and were centers of administration, trade, education, religion, and entertainment. Towns and cities were often laid out in a grid pattern, with streets intersecting at right angles. Some sections of the city held large, splendid houses of the wealthy, while others were crowded with the small houses of the poor.

Houses

Houses of rich and poor were of generally similar design, but varied in size, furnishings, decoration, and the amount of surrounding land devoted to courtyards and gardens. Urban houses generally were built of brick, with tile or thatched roofs. Each house was surrounded by a wall, with one or more buildings facing onto an interior courtyard. Houses of the wealthy often had many courtyards, and were filled with fine carved wooden furniture and decorated with works of art.

Chinese houses did not have central heating, but were heated by small portable char-

This flat-roofed house of sun-dried brick is built in a style typical of northwestern China.

A nineteenth century European engraving, showing various stages of planting and harvesting rice in China.

coal stoves. In winter, people wore heavy padded clothing indoors to keep warm. In northern China, the heat and smoke from the kitchen stove was often sent through ducts in a raised brick platform called a *kang* before it was expelled through a chimney. When the *kang* was covered with mattresses, it provided a warm place for sleeping.

Families

The family was the basic unit of Chinese society. Members of a family were expected to be loyal to and care for each other, to honor their ancestors, and to provide children to carry on the family name in future generations. Grandparents, parents, and children lived together, and younger family members owed respect and obedience to their elders. Children were taught to regard themselves as family members first, and individuals second. Chinese names reflect this: the family name is always written first, and the personal name second. The entire family was responsible for the behavior of its members, and honor or dishonor could be brought upon the entire family by any of its members.

Governments in ancient China tried to rule the country as one enormous, peaceful family. The emperor sometimes referred to himself as "the father and mother of the people."

Men

Chinese families were always headed by the eldest male member of the eldest generation. Sons owed absolute obedience to their fathers. For example, a son was expected to marry a wife picked out for him by his father,

A nineteenth century European engraving, showing a Chinese wedding ceremony. Marriages were arranged by families, and the bride and groom sometimes met for the first time at their own wedding.

whether he wanted to or not. In wealthy families, men could also have **concubines** of their own choice, but this was impossible for most people because they could not afford it.

Every Chinese family wanted to have at least one son, to carry on the family name and maintain the worship of the family's ancestors. Only sons could do this, because daughters married out of the family and became part of their husband's family after marriage.

In the families of farmers, shopkeepers, craftspersons, and other working people, men, women, and children all worked together. In wealthy families, however, men alone were responsible for the income of the family, while women spent most of their time at home and did not work to earn money.

Women

In traditional Chinese society, women had few rights. A woman was always expected to be obedient to men: first to her father, then to her husband, then if she became a widow, to her grown-up sons. Women married into their husbands' families, and had little contact with their own parents after marriage.

In wealthy families, servants and concubines had to obey the wife of the head of the family. Children of a man's concubines were regarded as the children of his official wife.

While men worked outside the house, women managed household affairs. Women also raised silkworms to produce silk, wove cloth and made clothing.

Children

Chinese children were treated with great love and affection, but also were taught to obey their elders without question. In poor families, children received little or no formal education, but only learned to do the work that their parents did. In families of moderate wealth, sons learned reading and arithmetic, while daughters learned homemaking skills. In wealthy families, sons were given a rigorous education in reading, writing, history, mathematics, and other subjects, to prepare them for official careers.

Food and Medicine

Since ancient times the Chinese have believed correctly that a proper diet is the basis of good health. Most people in China were farmers, whose main crop was grain of various kinds, and the Chinese diet was based on grain. Every Chinese meal is supposed to consist of *fan* and *cai*. *Fan* means "cooked grain," while *cai* literally means "vegetables," but in fact refers to all of the side dishes that might accompany a grain-based meal.

Rice is the favorite grain of people everywhere in China. But in northern China, where wheat and millet were the main grain crops, rice was expensive, and meals often were based on steamed buns, noodles, or pancakes, with side dishes of vegetables, soybean cakes (for protein), pickles, and occasionally meat, fish, or eggs. In southern China, rice was eaten at every meal.

Naturally, people's diets depended on their wealth. Poor people ate food that was plain and monotonous, with little meat or fish; wealthier people ate food that was richer, more varied, and prepared in more elaborate ways. Food was usually stir-fried or steamed, and ingredients were always cut into small pieces to make them convenient to eat with **chopsticks**. Most people in China ate two meals each day, in mid-morning and at dusk. Styles of cooking, with different spices and sauces, varied from one part of the country to another.

Tea was unknown in China in very ancient times, but was introduced from northern India sometime after the Han dynasty. It quickly became popular, and was usually drunk in the early morning and after meals. With meals, the Chinese preferred to drink rice wine, which was usually served warm.

Feasts

All important occasions in China, such as weddings, the birth of a son, funerals, and holidays, were celebrated with feasts, at which food was much more plentiful and elaborate than usual. Of course, the feasts of the rich were far more costly than those of the poor, but feasting was part of the lives of people of all classes. Banquet foods typically included a whole roasted duck or chicken, a whole fried fish, many vegetable dishes, and several soups, as well as sweet rice cakes and fruit. The feasts of the wealthy also included special, costly dishes such as bear's paws, shark's-fin soup, and roasted wild boar. Feasts were always accompanied by rice wine, and many toasts were drunk. Sometimes feasts were accompanied by music, and followed by dancing or other entertainment.

Medicine

The Chinese studied and practiced medicine from very early times. Chinese doctors be-

A Chinese bowl decorated with colored glazes made in the eleventh century A.D. during the Song dynasty.

lieved that health depended on a proper balance within the body of **yin** (dark, cool, moist, passive, female) and **yang** (bright, hot, dry active, male) forces, as well as types of activity symbolized by wood, fire, metal, earth, and water. Chinese medicine was aimed at maintaining these forces in proper balance, and correcting imbalances when they occurred.

Doctors learned to make many **herbal remedies** from plants. **Ginseng** was used as a general tonic, and willow bark (which contains a chemical similar to aspirin) was used to treat fevers. **Acupuncture** and **moxibustion** were also used to treat diseases. Acupuncture involves inserting thin needles into the body of the patient at specific places. In moxibustion, a special herbal powder is burned on the skin to produce blisters that, doctors believed, would draw off harmful forces.

Below: acupuncture chart showing the points where the needles are inserted, (Ming dynasty 1368–1644).

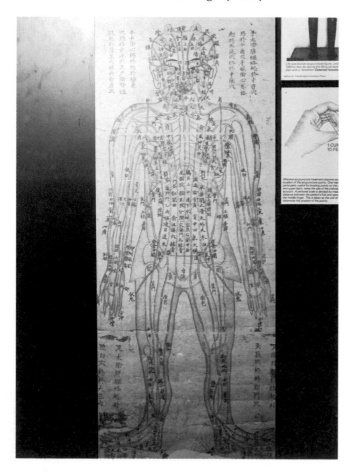

Above: sixteenth century ivory statue of the mythical physician Bian Qiao and the magician Zhang Shenkong.

Chinese doctors paid close attention to diet as a factor in health and disease. Traditional Chinese medicine developed successful treatments for a number of vitamin deficiency diseases, such as rickets and beriberi.

The earliest Chinese medical books date back to the late Zhou dynasty. Medical encyclopedias and books listing thousands of herbal remedies were written during the Tang, Song, and Qing dynasties. Medical students usually were trained by serving as apprentices to practicing physicians.

Buddhist and Daoist priests also sometimes treated diseases in ancient China. Instead of using medicines, they performed special religious ceremonies to drive evil forces out of a patient's body.

Clothes

Many different styles of clothing were worn in China during the thousands of years of its history. In ancient times, both men and women wore long robes tied with a sash. In the late Zhou dynasty, trousers and short jackets, copied from the horse-riding nomads of Central Asia, were adopted by Chinese men for hunting and fighting, and by both sexes for work clothes. Men and women of the upper classes usually wore long, flowing robes, while working people wore shorter and less bulky garments.

The clothing of ordinary people was most often made of cotton cloth. Hemp was used to make heavy work clothes, and linen-like cloth made from the fibers of the ramie plant was used for light summer clothing.

Wealthy people in traditional China usually wore clothing made of silk. Silk cloth was woven on large, complicated looms to produce a variety of brightly-colored patterns. Embroidery was also used to decorate silk clothing.

Imperial Dress

Men and women of imperial or noble rank wore special "dragon robes" that were long and embroidered with elaborate patterns. Specific details of color and design indicated the wearer's rank and status. The emperor's robes were yellow, and decorated with large dragons and other imperial symbols. Empresses wore similar robes decorated with phoenix birds.

Men

Men of the upper classes wore long robes. The robes of officials were decorated with squares of embroidery with special symbols that indicated their rank. They also wore special hats with ornaments of rank. Working class men wore loose, baggy jackets and trousers. In the winter, both robes and jackets were quilted and padded with cotton or silk fibers for warmth.

During most of Chinese history, men wore their hair long and tied up in elaborate top-knots. During the Qing dynasty, however, men were required to shave the front parts of their heads, and wear their remaining hair in a long pigtail. This was done as a sign of their loyalty to the Manchus who ruled China at the time.

A phoenix robe, which belonged to the empress dowager Ci Xi, the last empress of the Qing dynasty (1644–1911).

Women

Women of the upper classes were expected to dress modestly. They wore long robes with wide, long sleeves and high collars that buttoned at the neck. Such robes were often made of beautifully decorated silk cloth. Working class women wore jackets and trousers for ordinary wear, and long robes or skirts and tunics for special occasions.

Women wore their hair long, and devised many fancy hairstyles in which the hair was pinned up with large, jeweled hairpins. If they could afford it, Chinese women also liked to wear cosmetics, including facial powders, rouge, and eye make-up.

Above: early in the twentieth century foot binding was outlawed. Still, some elderly women bear the results of this traditional practice.

Below: portrait of an ancestor (seventeenth century painting on silk).

Bound Feet

During the Song dynasty, it became fashionable for women to have very small feet. The feet of young girls were made artificially small by wrapping them tightly in strips of cloth so that the toes curled under and the feet could not grow. For hundreds of years, until the practice was banned in the early twentieth century, most women were crippled by this cruel fashion. Only daughters of poor peasant families, who needed strong natural feet in order to work in the fields, were spared the pain of bound feet.

Colors

Plain white cloth was worn at funerals in China, and it was considered unlucky to wear white for any other occasion. Red was considered the color of happiness, and brides wore fancy red robes for their weddings. Only the emperor could wear yellow robes. Ordinary people usually wore black or dark blue clothing.

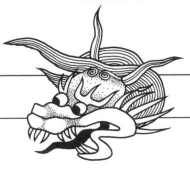

Religion and Rituals of the Chinese

China has sometimes been called the land of three religions: Confucianism, Daoism, and Buddhism. Confucianism and Daoism were purely Chinese teachings, while Buddhism was introduced into China from India during the late Han dynasty, in the first century A.D. But the situation is really more complicated than that. Chinese religious beliefs changed greatly over the course of 5,000 years of history, and the Chinese seldom drew a clear distinction between philosophy, religion, and folk belief.

Ancestor Worship

From the earliest times, the Chinese believed that the souls of people lived on after death. These souls needed to be cared for, worshipped, and sacrificed to, and that was the responsibility of their male descendants. Thus the family-centered religion of ancestor worship is the oldest and most fundamental religion of China. China's rulers built large temples for the worship of their imperial ancestors, and offered elaborate and expensive sacrifices to them. Ordinary people kept small shrines to their ancestors in their homes, and carefully kept the graves of their ancestors in good condition.

Confucianism

Confucius (Kong Fuzi, 551–479 B.C.) was a wise scholar who gave up an official career to become a teacher. His teachings said little

about reglion, but concentrated instead on good government, morality, and ethics. He taught that everyone has a duty to live the best and most moral life possible. He believed that the world would be peaceful and harmonious if everyone worshipped their ancestors properly, respected and obeyed their elders, and lived according to the principles of virtue, proper conduct, respect for others, loyalty, and trustworthiness.

In later times, Confucianism became the official policy of the government, and also took on religious dimensions. Government

This statue of the Buddha is carved into a cliff overlooking the junction of three rivers in Sichuan Province. At 223 feet (71 meters), it is the tallest Buddhist statue in the world. It was carved beginning in A.D. 713 by a monk who believed that the presence of the Buddha would calm the swift currents of the river and protect boatmen.

officials, from the emperor down to local magistrates, conducted worship services in public temples to the gods of heaven and earth, mountains and rivers, and other divinities.

Daoism

Daoism teaches that everything in the world reflects the **Dao**, "the way of heaven." The earliest Daoist philosophers lived shortly after the time of Confucius. They taught that people should live simply, free of ambition and striving, in order to have long and happy lives. During the Han dynasty, Daoist philosophy became joined with a variety of folk religions to become an organized religion with temples, priests, and a large number of gods and god-

desses. Daoists believed that it was possible for people to become immortal, by means of meditation, the taking of special medicines, and other practices.

Buddhism

Buddhism was founded by Siddhartha Gautama, a prince who was born in Nepal around 560 B.C. He taught that people went through endless cycles of births and rebirths, returning again and again to lives of suffering. From one life to the next, people carried a burden of **karma,** or responsibility for their actions. This cycle could be broken, he taught, if people would give up their desire for wordly things. Upon death, the soul of a fully enlightened person (called a Buddha) would not be reborn, but would live on in a state of eternal happiness called **nirvana.**

After Buddhism was introduced into China, over the centuries it was greatly affected by

Decorated porcelain plate showing Daoist sages admiring a painting of the yin/yang *symbol.*

Chinese culture. The beliefs and practices of Chinese Buddhism became quite different from those of India. Some sects of Chinese Buddhism taught that saints, called **bodhisattvas,** could help ordinary believers to achieve nirvana. Many Buddhist temples were built in China, where priests, monks, and nuns conducted worship services for believers.

Ceremonies and Rituals

Marriage

Young people in traditional China did not select their own mates, but rather married a boy or girl selected by their parents. Often a bride and groom would meet for the first time at their own wedding. The bride's family would provide a dowry of money, clothing, and household goods, while the groom's family would give presents to the family of the bride. On a lucky day selected with the help of astrologers, the bride, dressed in a red robe, would be carried in a sedan chair from her parents' house to the house of her husband. There, a marriage agreement would be signed, religious ceremonies were conducted, and a great banquet was held to celebrate the occasion.

Funerals

Funerals in China were grand, elaborate affairs. One of the most important duties of a son was to provide proper funerals for his parents when they died. Families would save money for years to be ready for the expense of a funeral, and often a fine coffin would be bought in advance to assure an elderly person that he or she would have a good funeral. On the day of death, the deceased would be dressed in fine clothing and placed in the coffin. Relatives, dressed in plain white mourning clothes, would show their respect by **kowtowing**, that is, kneeling and knocking their foreheads on the floor.

A grave site would be selected with the help

Funerary figure of a woman on horseback, from the Tang dynasty A.D. 618—906.

of magicians who specialized in finding lucky places for graves. The coffin would be carried to the tomb in a large procession. The family would walk behind the coffin, followed by musicians and people carrying flower wreaths and offerings. In ancient times, clay and bronze offerings were buried with the dead person, but in later times that practice was discontinued. Instead, paper money and paper models of houses, servants, clothing, and other goods would be burned to accompany the soul of the departed person into the afterlife.

25

Obeying the Law

Government

In ancient times, China consisted of many feudal states, but beginning with the Qin dynasty in 221 B.C., it was united under a new form of imperial government. The whole country was divided into provinces, which were subdivided into districts and counties. The emperor selected ministers to help him rule the central government, and appointed governors and magistrates to rule the provinces, districts, and counties. These officials were selected according to merit. In the Han dynasty, a system of written examinations was created to select the best officials, and this system continued to be used for more than 2,000 years.

The Chinese regarded their country as "The Middle Kingdom" or "All Under Heaven," and claimed that the emperor's mandate from heaven gave him the right to rule the entire known world. The emperor's responsibility was to run a government that was fair and which protected and encouraged the common people. When the emperor or his officals governed poorly, special officials called **censors** had the duty of criticizing the government and suggesting reforms. When government was especially bad, popular rebellions broke out. Sometimes a new leader would arise, overthrow the ruling dynasty, and establish a new dynasty in its place.

Law

Confucius believed that if a country was well governed, law would be unnecessary. People would naturally behave properly if their families and the government taught them how to be good and set a good example. A rival school of thought, the Legalists, taught that people were naturally bad, and would only be good if they were governed by strict laws.

During imperial times, the Chinese government adopted a compromise position, and tried to rule both by setting a good example and by law. District and county magistrates played a key role in this. Their jobs included conducting rituals at official temples, collecting taxes, and enforcing the law.

The government expected people to settle minor disputes on their own. In cases of serious crimes, the magistrate would investigate, order the police to arrest the criminal, and conduct a trial. If found guilty, a criminal could be fined, beaten, exiled, or sentenced to death. A person who falsely accused someone else of a crime would be punished as if he had committed the crime himself.

Interior of the Palace of Heavenly Purity, which is inside the Forbidden City in Beijing. The emperor held formal audiences in the Palace of Heavenly Purity.

Writing It Down: Recording Things

Chinese words are written in symbols called characters or ideograms. The earliest Chinese characters were simple pictures representing things or concepts. But they soon evolved into a more complex form. Several thousand Chinese characters are in common use today, and each character represents a single word. To create new vocabulary, words can be combined to form compounds. For example, "electric speech" means "telephone."

The earliest surviving Chinese writing is found on bones and tortoise shells that date back to the Shang dynasty, around 1300 B.C. These inscriptions are records of **divinations.** Shang rulers asked questions to the gods to get advice. Bones or tortoise shells were heated until they cracked, and the cracks were read by priests to find the answers to the questions. The questions and answers were then engraved onto the bones as a record.

In later times, inscriptions were carved on stone tablets or cast on bronze vessels. Books were written on narrow strips of bamboo tied together in rolls, or on pieces of silk cloth. One of China's greatest contributions to world civilization is paper, which was invented in the first century B.C. Paper, made of mulberry bark and other plant fibers, made books much cheaper and more widely available. Ink was made from soot and glue, and formed into small dry sticks which were ground with water on special stones when a supply of ink was needed.

Printing

Printing was invented in China sometime between the fourth and the seventh centuries A.D. Words were carved (in reverse, as mirror images) on smooth blocks of wood, so that the words were raised above the surface of the block. The raised characters would be patted with an ink-soaked pad of cloth. A sheet of paper was then placed over the block and brushed with a dry brush, transferring the ink to the paper. Each sheet of paper was then peeled off the block. Sheets were then glued together to make scrolls, or folded and sewn together to make books. The earliest surviving scroll printed using this methods was a Buddhist religious text, the *Diamond Sutra*.

Moveable Type

Moveable type was invented in China in the eleventh century A.D., long before Gutenberg

The Diamond Sutra, *printed in A.D. 868, is the world's earliest dated printed book.*

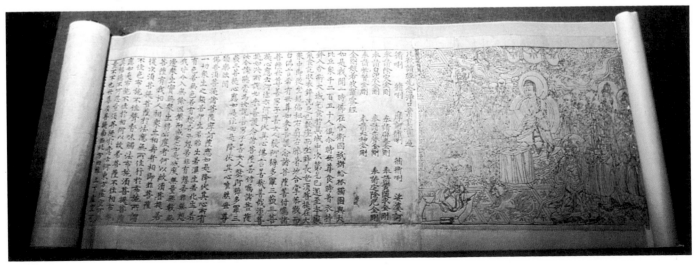

made the same invention in Europe. Single characters carved from wood or made from baked clay were arranged in order on an iron framework, and used to print sheets of paper. The characters could then be removed and reused. This was more flexible than carving each whole page from a wooden block. But because the Chinese language uses thousands of characters, typesetting was a slow and difficult task, and moveable type did not entirely replace wood block printing.

The Calendar and Time

In part because the Chinese believed in astrology, or the influence of the heavens on human affairs, Chinese astronomy reached a high level of development in ancient times. The emperor's official Bureau of Astronomy was re-

sponsible for producing an accurate calendar that showed not only the days of the year, but also the phases of the moon and the movements of the planets.

The Chinese calendar used both a solar year of 365 1/4 days and twelve lunar months of 29 days each. Extra months were added occasionally to keep the two systems in line. Each day was divided into 12 double hours, which were divided into 100 minutes. During the Song and Yuan dynasties, a number of large water-powered clocks were made for use in the imperial palace. Most people, however, used sundials to tell the time.

Weights and Measures

One of the most important achievements of the Qin dynasty, which unified China under imperial rule in 221 B.C., was to create a standard system of weights and measures for the whole country. The basic unit of measurement was the foot, slightly longer than a modern foot, divided into ten inches. The basic unit of weight was the *jin*, about two pounds or one kilogram.

Numbers

Like Roman numerals, the Chinese characters for numbers are very awkward for doing arithmetic. In ancient times, counting rods were used instead of written calculations. Later the **abacus** was invented, which made arithmetic very fast and simple.

Inscribed wooden strip from the Han dynasty. The poem reads:
The sun is hidden from view by dark clouds,
The moon is concealed by sand swept up by the wind.
I follow the waters of the Meng River, like the Yellow River and the Yangtse.
The waters flow and roll in waves.
I did not climb up when I reached Bi
For the gate of heaven is narrow so I walked to the Peng pool,
How could I climb up there without help?...
It is difficult to pass the gate.

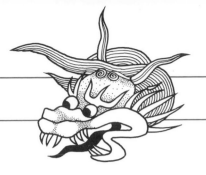

Chinese Legends and Literature

From very early times the Chinese have placed a high value on written literature. No one could become a government official without being well educated and then passing a difficult series of written examinations. Members of the upper classes were expected to have a thorough knowledge of history and literature, and to be skilled at writing essays and poetry.

The earliest Chinese literature dates from the mid-Zhou dynasty. Some important early books were the *Classic of History,* a collection of ancient historical documents, the *Classic of Poetry,* and the *Book of Changes,* a manual of fortune-telling. These works contain some ancient myths, but much of early Chinese mythology has been lost. Confucius and his followers believed that it was important to concentrate on government and human af-

Limestone relief depicting the pilgrimage of the boy Sudhana. Buddhist legends from India became popular in China.

fairs, and they were less interested in tales of ancient gods and heroes.

Types of Chinese Literature

The works of Confucius and his disciples were regarded by the Chinese as their most important literature. For anyone to pass the official examinations, it was necessary to have memorized these books. History was also highly valued. Every dynasty had a duty to write a complete official history of the previous dynasty, and many works of history were written by private individuals as well.

Poetry was considered the most beautiful form of literature. Many famous poets lived during the Tang dynasty, which is often called the golden age of Chinese poetry. The three best poets of that age, Li Bo, Du Fu, and Bo Zhuyi, are as highly regarded in China as Shakespeare is in the English-speaking world.

Gods and Sages

The ancient Chinese did not believe in a creator god. Instead, they believed that the world simply evolved from its original formless state. People came into being, along with animals, plants, and everything else in the world. But these first people lived lives that were not much better than animals, so gods and sages appeared to teach them how to be civilized. *Shen Nong,* the "Divine Farmer," and *Hou Ji,* "Lord Millet," taught people how to plow the fields and plant crops. They also showed people which wild plants were useful as medicines. Later Shen Nong was worshipped as the God of Medicine.

Huang Di, the "Yellow Emperor" invented the calendar, metal-working, and many other things. His wife invented the practice of raising silkworms to obtain silk, and taught women how to use looms to weave cloth. *Fu Xi* invented writing and divination. *Shang Di,* "High Lord," was the chief god, who governed heaven.

At first there were ten suns, which rested in the branches of magical mulberry trees in the east and west; each day *Xihe* drove one of them in a golden chariot across the sky. One day all ten suns came out together, and threatened to burn up the world. *Yi the Archer* shot down nine of them with his bow, and after that the one remaining sun had to travel across the sky every day.

Two monsters, *Kong Kong* and *Zhuan Xu,* fought to see which one would become emperor, and they knocked over one of the eight pillars that separated heaven and earth. *Nü Gua,* the wife of the god *Fu Xi,* repaired the pillar with the leg of a jade turtle. Fu Xi and Nü Gua had human heads and bodies, but long tails like the tails of dragons.

Xi Wang Mu, the Queen Mother of the West, was a very powerful goddess. She was very beautiful, but when she became angry her face became ferocious, with teeth like those of a tiger. The garden of her palace had a pool of turquoise water, which was surrounded by an orchard of magical peach trees. Whoever ate one of the peaches would become immortal. Xi Wang Mu also had some magical immortality pills. One day a young goddess name *Heng E,* who was the wife of Yi the Archer, tried to steal some of those magical pills. She was caught, and was banished to the moon.

The era of the first gods lasted for many centuries. Then the gods allowed a human to become the emperor of the world. This first emperor, whose name was *Yao,* was no ordinary human, however. He was virtuous and wise, and ruled for over one hundred years. As he was dying, he looked for the wisest man in the kingdom to be his successor. A very good but humble man named *Shun* was found fishing along the bank of a river. Yao offered the throne to him, but he refused, saying that he was not worthy. But after Yao insisted, Shun realized that it was his duty to become emperor, and so he became the second sage-king of China's legendary golden age.

During Shun's reign, a tribe of people called the San Miao rebelled against him. Shun defeated them and drove them from the empire. But their wickedness caused the balance of heaven and earth to be disrupted, and it began to rain for many days until the world was covered by a great flood.

Shun first asked his minister *Gun* to tame the flood. But Gun's plan was to steal magical earth from the gods to build dams to contain the water. The gods punished him by turning him to stone and leaving him on a mountainside. After three years, Gun's son *Yü the Great* sprang forth full-grown from his body. Following the trails left in the mud by the tails of dragons, Yü the Great dug channels to drain away the water. China's great rivers began to flow through those channels, and the dry land appeared again. When Shun died, Yü the Great became the founder of the Xia Dynasty. Thus the age of gods and sage-kings came to an end, and human history began.

Magical Animals

Chinese mythology also tells many stories of magical animals. Dragons in Chinese mythology were powerful and sometimes fierce, but they were not evil, as in Western mythology. Instead, dragons brought rain and other blessings. Only kings and emperors could control dragons. Many people believed that if a dragon were seen on earth, it meant that the founder of a new dynasty was about to be born.

The phoenix was a magical bird that lived in the south and was a symbol of fire. It was also associated with music. In later times, the phoenix became a symbol of the empress, as the dragon was a symbol of the emperor.

Turtles were also believed to have magical powers in ancient China. Fu Xi invented writing after he examined the mysterious patterns on the back of a turtle that emerged from the Lo River. In the divination rituals of the Shang kings, the bottom shells of turtles were cracked by heat to give answers to questions that were asked to gods and royal ancestors.

Another magical animal was the *qilin*, a kind of unicorn with a tiger's head and a horse's body. It protected virtuous people.

Between the Han dynasty and the Tang dynasty, hundreds of Buddhist scriptures were translated from Indian languages into Chinese. Many additional religious works were written by Chinese believers in Buddhism, and religious Daoism also developed a large body of sacred texts. Through the ages, Chinese writers produced thousands of books on subjects of all kinds, from astronomy to agriculture, and from folk customs to philosophy.

All of these works were written in Classical Chinese, a formal language used only by well-educated people. Beginning in the Song dynasty, short stories, plays, and novels were written in a less formal style that was closer to the everyday spoken language. But such works were considered simply light entertainment, and were not taken seriously as literature by most educated people.

A nineteenth century ivory figure of Shen Nong, the Chinese god of agriculture and medicine.

Art and Architecture

Bronze

Magnificent bronze vessels, used in sacrificial rituals, were made during the Shang and Zhou dynasties. The vessels were cast from molten bronze in clay molds, with intricate and finely designed surface decorations. These bronze vessels are the finest surviving examples of ancient Chinese art. In later times, bronze continued to be used, but bronze objects declined in both importance and quality as tastes and religious rituals changed.

Jade

Jade is a general term for two types of stone, jadite and nephrite. Both were used in China beginning in the New Stone Age to make ceremonial objects and jewelry. Jade is extremely hard, and cannot be carved with metal tools. It must be ground into shape using wooden tools and sand. Jade was sometimes placed in tombs, because it was believed to protect bodies from decay. In later times, jade was used to make bowls, artificial flowers, and other decorative objects.

Pottery and Porcelain

Red clay pottery decorated with black designs was made in ancient China as much as 6,000 years ago. In later ages, Chinese potters con-

Above: Chinese pottery jar, eleventh–twelfth centuries A.D.

tinually experimented to find new ways of making harder and finer pottery vessels, decorated with colored glazes. Tang dynasty "Three colored" pottery was made with green, beige and brown glazes. In the Song dynasty, true porcelain was made of pure white china clay. During the Ming and Qing dynasties porcelain decoration became increasingly fancy, with blue-and-white or multicolored glazes.

Calligraphy and Painting

Calligraphy, the art of writing beautifully, was regarded as the most important of all arts in China. The technique of writing Chinese characters on silk or paper with a soft, pointed brush was adopted for painting as well. No Chinese person could be considered well-educated without being adept at both calligraphy and painting.

Below: bronze tripod vessel made during the Shang dynasty, twelfth–tenth centuries B.C.

The Forbidden City in Bejing was built in the early fifteenth century.

The Song dynasty is generally considered the greatest age of Chinese painting. Landscape paintings were especially admired, but Chinese artists also painted flowers, bamboo, birds, and many other subjects.

Lacquer

Lacquer, a Chinese invention, is made from the sap of the lac tree. The sap was mixed with colors, usually red or black, and used to coat the surface of bowls, boxes, and other objects made of wood, cloth, or even paper. Lacquer is very durable and is not affected by heat or moisture.

Textiles

The art of weaving was very highly developed in ancient China. Special looms, called **drawlooms**, had been invented by the time of the Han dynasty to weave complex patterns in silk cloth. Such textiles were used not only to make clothing but also bedspreads, cushion covers, and decorative wall hangings.

Architecture

Palaces, temples, and other large public buildings in ancient China were built on raised stone platforms. They had wooden columns, made from the trunks of large trees, that supported strong wooden roof brackets. These brackets distributed the weight of the buildings' heavy tile roofs. Thin walls of brick or plaster were then built between the columns. This style of construction made buildings slightly flexible, so that they would not collapse in China's frequent earthquakes. However, being made of wood, buildings were very vulnerable to fire.

The roofs of Chinese buildings were a very prominent part of their design. Some buildings had double or triple roofs, with eaves that swept upwards in graceful curves. Roof tiles were often glazed in bright colors. Yellow tiles were used only on imperial buildings.

Chinese buildings were often surrounded by walls, which enclosed courtyards and gardens as well as the buildings themselves. The layout of buildings and courtyards within a walled compound was characterized by order and symmetry.

Going Places: Transportation, Exploration, and Communication

Throughout the history of imperial China, the Chinese traded with distant neighbors. Camel caravans carried silk, porcelain, and other goods to the Near East, and ships brought goods from Persia, India, and Southeast Asia to ports along China's coast. But because of China's vast size, most trade was conducted within the country, rather than abroad.

Waterways

Beginning in the Zhou dynasty, boats and barges were used to carry grain and other heavy goods on China's rivers, and canals were built to make such transportation easier. During the Sui dynasty (A.D. 589–618), the Grand Canal was built, linking Hangzhou on the east-central coast with the inland capital of Chang'an—a distance of over 1,000 miles (1,600 kilometers). Locks allowed the canal to cross hills along the way. During the Ming dynasty, the Grand Canal was rebuilt to go northward to the new capital at Beijing.

Chinese ships ranged from small **sampans** to large, ocean-going **junks**. During the fifteenth century, the Ming government sponsored expeditions of "treasure ships"—huge, multi-masted junks, over 400 feet (1,200 meters) long— that explored the Indian Ocean as far west as the coast of Africa. Later, however, the government lost interest in long-distance trade and exploration, and the ships were abandoned.

A nineteenth century painting of a Chinese junk. By the ninth century, Chinese junks were making safe voyages to India. By the fifteenth century, junks had become the largest, strongest, and most seaworthy ships in the world.

Roads

In northern China, the dry terrain made roads more important than waterways. A network of roads linked cities and towns throughout northern China, and extended into the south where waterways were unavailable. Roads ranged from narrow tracks suitable only to pack animals and people on foot, to stone-paved highways used by wagons drawn by horses or oxen. Relay stations were maintained along important roads to provide fresh horses for official messengers.

Chinese engineers grew very skillful at building strong, graceful stone bridges that carried roads across rivers and canals.

The famous Silk Route was not really a road, but rather a system of caravan trails that led from oasis to oasis across the deserts of Central Asia.

Music, Dancing, and Recreation

Music and Dance

Chinese music has a long history, and has always been regarded as an important part of ritual and education. Confucius believed that the formal, solemn music of rituals had a good moral influence on people, but that "improper" music could make people behave badly. Ancient Chinese music was based mainly on drums, bells, gongs, and flutes. Religious rituals included dancing as well as music. During imperial times, Daoism and Buddhism developed their own distinctive styles of music.

Stringed instruments, such as the viol, the zither, and the lute, became popular after the Han dynasty. In addition to poetry, calligraphy, and painting, music was an essential part of the education of members of China's upper classes. Poetry was often sung or chanted to musical accompaniment. Social dancing with partners was unknown in China, but female dancers were often called upon to entertain at banquets and celebrations.

Theater

From ancient times, troupes of performers performed plays in marketplaces or temple courtyards for public entertainment. Buddhist temples sometimes staged religious plays to teach people about the Buddha.

Chinese plays were always accompanied by instrumental music, and much of the dialogue was sung. Plays were performed on a simple stage, but actors wore fancy costumes and facial makeup. Few props were used, and instead pantomime was employed to indicate the setting of the action.

Recreation

Popular Chinese games included kick-ball, kite flying, wrestling, archery, fencing, horse racing, and cockfights. Jugglers, acrobats, and storytellers drew large crowds in marketplaces. The Chinese were fond of board games, including several versions of chess. Mah-jong, a form of rummy played with small ivory tiles rather than cards, was a popular form of gambling game. Dogs, songbirds, crickets, and goldfish were kept as pets.

Festivals

The Chinese calendar repeated in a cycle of twelve years, with each year named after an animal: ox, rat, horse, and so on. The New

Opera singers performing a traditional Chinese opera in the Gardens of Performing Arts. In the foreground are the musicians. The performers' costumes are elaborate compared to the simple sets.

Year's Festival was the most important holiday during the year. People set off firecrackers to drive away evil spirits, held banquets with special New Year's foods, and visited friends and relatives.

Other important festivals included *Qing Ming*, which celebrated the return of spring, and All Soul's Day, in late summer, a time of remembrance for a family's ancestors. In early summer, Dragon Boat races were held on China's rivers. In the fall, harvest festivals were held in the countryside.

Silk scroll from the tenth century A.D. depicting musicians at court.

Wars and Battles

Throughout history, Chinese governments faced two main military threats. The first was from the nomadic herdsmen, such as the Mongols, on the northern frontier. These nomads often tried to expand their grazing lands by conquering parts of northern China. Sometimes they even tried to conquer and rule China itself. The second threat was from civil war, popular rebellions, and banditry within China itself.

Early Warfare

In the feudal era of the Shang and Zhou dynasties, wars were fought by small armies. Noblemen fought from chariots with swords and battle-axes, while foot soldiers supported them with swords, bows, and spears. By the Warring States period in the later Zhou dynasty, armies had grown larger and more dangerous. Large-scale infantry formations grew more important, and the crossbow was adopted as the main infantry weapon. Armies were supported by troops of cavalry armed with bows and spears. Chariots were used only as command vehicles, not for actual fighting.

By the Qin dynasty, soldiers wore heavy armor made of leather covered with small rectangles of bronze. Crossbows, able to shoot a short, bronze-tipped arrow powerfully enough to pierce armor or kill a horse, were mass-produced for military use. Large numbers of horses were raised for military use, and the Chinese adopted the cavalry tactics of their nomadic neighbors to the north.

Officers

In feudal times, military officers were members of the nobility. They wore brightly-colored robes in battle, and carried bronze weapons decorated with gold, turquoise, and jade. In the Qin and Han dynasties, officers were often promoted from the ranks of ordinary soldiers for showing exceptional skill and leadership ability in battle. In later ages, military examina-

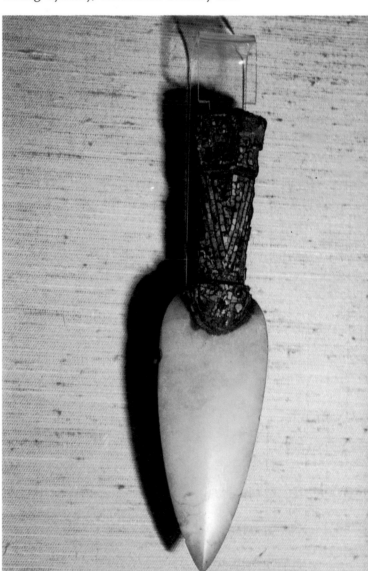

Jade spearhead with bronze and turquoise from the Shang dynasty, thirteenth century B.C.

tions were used to recruit and select officers for their fighting skills and knowledge of military theory.

Gunpowder

Gunpowder was invented in China in the ninth century A.D. During the eleventh and twelfth centuries the Chinese invented many gunpowder weapons, including fire arrows, exploding rockets, flamethrowers, and bombs hurled by catapults. Such weapons were used not only against armies and walled cities, but by warships that fought on the rivers of southern China and along the coast.

Cannons and mortars were in use in China by the fourteenth century. Nevertheless, most Chinese armies continued to rely on crossbows, swords, and spears. Meanwhile, Europeans learned about gunpowder from the Chinese, and developed gunpowder technology further than the Chinese had done. When Chinese and European armies fought during the nineteenth century, the Europeans were able to win easily because of their superior weapons.

Warrior from the tomb of the first emperor of the Qin dynasty. From these figures it is possible to know what battle clothes the warriors wore.

Chinese Inventions and Special Skills

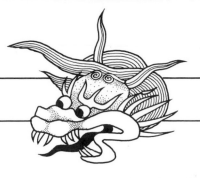

China has been the source of important inventions and skills throughout its history. These Chinese inventions and many others have helped to make modern civilization possible all over the world.

Silk

The making of silk fabric from fibers produced by silkworms was invented in China as early as the third millennium B.C. Silkworm raising and silk weaving were the work of women. Silkworms—really the caterpillar of a certain kind of moth—were placed in wooden frames, kept warm in a special part of the house, and fed with mulberry leaves. When the caterpillars were fully grown, they spun a cocoon of silk around their bodies as they turned into pupae. The cocoons were collected and boiled before the pupae turned into moths. The silk fibers were then unwrapped from the cocoons, combed, spun into thread, and woven into cloth.

Beginning in the Han dynasty, large quantities of silk cloth were exported from China to the Near East and the Roman Empire along the Silk Route. For many centuries, only the Chinese knew how to make silk. in the early Tang dynasty, Christian missionaries from Syria brought some silkworms back from China when they returned to the Near East. Silk production then spread to Persia and Italy.

Astronomy

Throughout history, Chinese astronomers kept careful records of their observations of the heavens. In addition to compiling calendars, they recorded sightings of comets, meteors, eclipses, sunspots, and supernovae.

Chinese astronomers also made bronze instruments to help them with their observations. An armillary sphere, which is a nest of rings showing the horizon, the zenith, and the paths of the sun, moon and other heavenly bodies across the sky, was invented in China during the Han dynasty. In the 1280s A.D., the Mongol emperor Kublai Khan built the finest observatory that had ever been seen, equipped with many different kinds of instruments.

Metalworking

Bronze was used in China beginning in the second millennium B.C. Chinese bronze workers quickly reached a high level of technical and artistic skill. Bronze, an alloy of copper and tin, was melted and poured into clay molds to produce vessels, weapons, and other things.

Chinese metalworkers used similar methods to produce the world's earliest cast iron during the mid-Zhou dynasty. Large numbers of iron plows, hoes, and other tools were made inexpensively in reusable metal molds. This enabled Chinese workers to clear and work their fields more efficiently, and to make canals, roads, and buildings more easily.

Porcelain

Simple clay pottery was made throughout the ancient world, but the Chinese developed the art of pottery making to a level that no other ancient civilization achieved. They developed many different kinds of glazes, and built kilns that could reach the high temperatures needed to make the hard, strong pottery known as porcelain. The earliest type of porcelain was produced during the Han dynasty. By the Song dynasty, pure white porcelain was made in large quantities and exported as far away as Indonesia, India, Persia, and even East Africa. Chinese porcelain became very popular in Europe, where the secret of porcelain making was learned only in the eighteenth century.

Casts of wooden type with Mongolian words, A.D. 1300.

Paper

Paper was first made in China around 100 B.C., and its use had become widespread by the later Han dynasty. Paper was usually made from mulberry tree bark, though cotton rags, bamboo, and straw were also sometimes used. The raw material was pounded to separate the fibers, which were mixed with water. A thin sheet of fiber was collected on a bamboo mat held in a wooden frame. The fiber mat was then removed, pressed, and dried to make a sheet of paper. By providing a cheap and durable material for writing, paper helped to make education more widespread in China, and eventually throughout the world.

Printing

Printing, invented in China sometime between the fourth and seventh centuries A.D., was first used to reproduce short Buddhist religious texts that were carried as charms by believers. Later, long scrolls and books were produced, first by wood-block printing and then, beginning in the eleventh century, by using moveable type. Inexpensive printed books became widely available in China during the Song dynasty.

Printing was re-invented in Europe around the 1430s by Johann Gutenberg, who may have been influenced by travelers' tales about printed books in China.

Gunpowder

Gunpowder was discovered in China during the Tang dynasty, possibly by accident. The first written reference to gunpowder, in a Tang book about chemistry, says, "If you mix charcoal, nitrate, and saltpeter together, it might explode and burn your beard."

The Chinese quickly learned the usefulness of this dangerous mixture. They developed many different recipes for gunpowder, depending on whether it was to be used for fireworks, explosive weapons, flamethrowers, military rockets, or cannon.

The Compass

Compass needles carved from pieces of magnetite (a magnetic iron ore) were used in China as early as the Han dynasty. For a long time they were used mainly to lay out sites for graves, temples, and other structures. By the eleventh century, thin magnetized iron needles were used to make navigational compasses. Such compasses helped Chinese sailors to travel out of sight of land without getting lost. Chinese-style compasses were used by Columbus and other Spanish and Portuguese navigators in their voyages of exploration.

Other Inventions

The wheelbarrow, an efficient type of horse harness, and the water-powered clock (the ancestor of later European weight-driven clocks) were all invented in China. Deep drilling with derricks, a long flexible drillstring, and iron drill bits— the same basic technique used for oil wells today—was used as early as the Han dynasty to drill wells for brine (to produce salt) and natural gas.

Why the Civilization Declined

China produced one of the most long-lasting and stable civilizations that the world has ever seen. Many of the basic characteristics of Chinese civilization were established during the Shang and Zhou dynasties. The imperial form of government set up by the Qin dynasty in 221 B.C. evolved considerably over time, but lasted without fundamental change for more than 2,200 years.

Under the Ming and Qing dynasties (1368–1911), China ruled the largest and richest empire in the world. Yet the prosperity and stability of the Chinese empire blinded its rulers to crucial changes that were taking place both within the country and in the outside world—changes that finally would lead to the collapse of traditional China.

China's population increased from about 250 million at the beginning of the Ming to 450 million at the end of the Qing. This increase put pressure on land use, food resources, and government administration. Popular rebellions brought about the end of the Ming dynasty in 1644, and more rebellions disrupted China in the mid-nineteenth century.

Moreover, the ruling class of China grew too satisfied with its own wealth and power. The inventiveness, curiosity, and energy of earlier years were often replaced by corruption and extravagance. Meanwhile, the Scientific Revolution and the Industrial Revolution helped Europe advance quickly while China grew stagnant.

During the early nineteenth century, more and more Europeans came to China to buy silk, porcelain, tea, and other goods, and to sell opium to the Chinese. When China tried to limit this trade, the Europeans responded with war, and won easily. Internally weak and under pressure from European trade, warfare, and new ideas, the government could not cope with its problems. The last emperor of China was driven from his throne in 1911, and a republican form of government was set up.

Young school children in China, today.

Glossary

Abacus A device consisting of beads strung on wires set in a frame, used for counting and making calculations.

Acupuncture A Chinese medical treatment whereby long, sharp metal needles are inserted into the underlying tissue of the skin at carefully chosen points to cure various ailments.

Astrology A belief that the movement of heavenly bodies has an influence on human affairs. In China, belief in astrology led to great advances in the science of astronomy, as observations were made and records were kept of the movements of the sun, moon, and planets, and of unusual occurrences such as eclipses, comets, meteors, and supernovae.

Buddha In Buddhist religion, a perfectly enlightened being who, upon death, escapes from the cycle of karma and rebirth and enters into the eternal state of nirvana.

Bodhisattva In Buddhist religion, a perfectly enlightened being who chooses to postpone becoming a Buddha in order to assist others in gaining salvation; a Buddhist saint.

Calligraphy The art of writing beautifully. In China, calligraphy was regarded as the highest of the arts, and famous calligraphers were considered supreme artists. The techniques of Chinese calligraphy, involving writing words with ink and a soft brush, also formed the basis for painting.

Carp A large freshwater fish which in China was often raised in ponds and used for food.

Censor In imperial Chinese government, an official whose job was to criticize the emperor and other officials for mistakes or misconduct.

Chopsticks A pair of thin sticks made of bamboo, wood or ivory, and used by the Chinese as eating utensils.

Concubine A secondary wife who lives in a man's house without being legally married to him.

Delta The part of a river near the sea where the river slows down and fans out over a plain, dropping sediment and building new land. The richest areas of Chinese agriculture are in the deltas of the Yellow and Yangtse rivers.

Divination A practice which attempts to discover hidden truths or reveal the future by magical means. In ancient China, divination was practiced by reading cracks in bones and turtle shells, or by consulting the lines of the *Book of Changes*.

Dao In Chinese philosophy and religion, "the way of heaven," the right and proper form of action or behavior. Sometimes spelled "Tao."

Drawloom A type of loom used to weave intricately patterned fabrics. It was invented in China for silk weaving, and was later introduced into Europe during the Middle Ages.

Dynasty A hereditary ruling house or family. Founders of Chinese dynasties normally took power following a popular rebellion. Their successors ruled until that dynasty too was overthrown.

Emperor The supreme ruler of an empire, that is, a realm that includes a large area and governs people of different languages and cultures. The emperors of China claimed that the Mandate of Heaven gave them the right to rule All Under Heaven, meaning the entire world as they knew it.

Examination system A system, begun during the Han dynasty, of recruiting government officials by means of written examinations.

Feudalism A political system in which a ruler exercises power through nobles who govern their own territories but are personally loyal to him.

Ginseng A plant with aromatic root, used extensively in Chinese medicine.

Hemp A tall, weed-like plant, sometimes cultivated for its fibers which are used for making cloth and rope.

Herbal remedies Medicines made of substances from plants. Chinese medicine relied heavily on herbal remedies to treat diseases.

Jade Jadite or nephrite, types of stone highly valued in ancient China for their beauty and hardness, and used to make jewelry and other ornamental objects. Jade was believed to promote immortality and to protect dead bodies from decay.

Junk A type of Chinese sailing vessel with a high stern and projecting bow and one or more masts. Junks carried rectangular sails made of cloth with bamboo slats. Large junks were highly seaworthy and capable of long ocean voyages.

Karma The Buddhist belief that actions in one's present life and previous lives affect one's rebirth in future lives. Every action brings a reward or punishment in the future.

Kowtow A Chinese way of showing reverence and worship by kneeling before a person or object and touching one's forehead to the ground.

Loess A type of yellowish, fine-grained, wind-blown soil, highly fertile if irrigated, that covers much of northern China.

Magistrate In the imperial Chinese government, an official who governed a district or county, and was responsible for law enforcement, tax collection, public ceremonies, and other administrative duties.

Mandarin A Portuguese word used to denote any member of the imperial Chinese government. Mandarins were organized as a civil service, with nine grades of rank.

Mandate of Heaven In ancient Chinese belief, the right granted by the supreme gods to a king or emperor authorizing him to rule the empire. The Mandate of Heaven was handed down by a dynastic founder to his descendants until the dynasty was overthrown.

Millet A type of edible grain. Millet was the earliest grain plant domesticated in China, during the New Stone Age.

Moxibustion A medical procedure used to treat ailments by burning pellets of vegetable fiber on the surface of the skin.

Nirvana In Buddhism, the eternal state of release from suffering and from the cycle of rebirth governed by karma.

Paddy field A field in which rice is grown. It can be flooded when the rice is planted, and drained for the harvest.

Pagoda A multi-storied tower often built as part of the buildings of a Buddhist temple. Pagodas originated in India, but developed a unique style under the influence of Chinese architecture.

Ramie A plant native to East Asia, raised for its fibers which were used to make a linen-like textile.

Reincarnation The belief that the soul, upon the death of the body, is reborn in a new body.

Sampan A type of small Chinese boat that could be either sailed or propelled by oars. Sampans were usually used on rivers, canals, or in sheltered coastal waters.

Silk Route A network of caravan trails extending from northwestern China to the Near East, along which silk and other goods were traded between China and the western world.

Yamen A complex of buildings containing the offices and official residence of a Chinese magistrate.

Yin/Yang In Chinese religion and philosophy, the theory that everything has a dual nature: cold/hot, female/male, low/high, and so on.

The Chinese: Some Famous People and Places

YUN'GANG AND LONGMEN CAVES

Many Chinese Buddhists believed that they could receive religious merit by donating Buddhist statues or sacred scriptures to temples. In many parts of China, artificial caves were created in cliffs where worshippers could pay to have statues carved in grottoes in the rock. Two of the most famous of these cave-temples are at Yun'gang, in Shaanxi Province, and Longmen, in Henan Province, both in northern China.

In both cases, the cave temples were founded in the Northern Wei dynasty in the fifth century A.D., during China's period of political disunion. Each site contains dozens of caves, with Buddhist statues ranging from a few inches high to ones many times the size of a person. The carving of statues continued until the early Song dynasty. Many of the statues, and especially the earlier ones, are regarded as among the greatest masterpieces of Chinese stone sculpture.

THE FORBIDDEN CITY

Beijing became China's capital under the Mongol Yuan dynasty, and continued in use as the capital under the Ming and Qing dynasties. Imperial palaces, gardens, and administrative buildings were built as a walled city-within-a-city, where entry was prohibited to unauthorized persons. The main ceremonial halls of the Forbidden City are regarded as among the finest examples of Chinese architecture.

LAOZI

Laozi lived during the sixth century B.C., around the same time as Confucius. Very little is known about his life. He apparently was a librarian at the court of the Zhou kings, and he is regarded as the founder of the Daoist school of philosophy. The Daoist sacred book, the *Dao De Jing* ("The Way and Its Power"), is said to have been written by Laozi, but in fact it probably was not written until several hundred years after his death.

By the late Han dynasty, Laozi had become a mythical person who was regarded as a great Daoist sage. He was worshipped as a god by believers in the Daoist religion, and many legends developed about his life.

MENCIUS

Mencius (Mengzi) was born in 371 B.C. His father died when he was three, and he was raised and educated by his mother (who was used in China as an example of a perfect mother). He became a fellow student of the grandson of Confucius, from who he learned about the teachings of Confucius. Later he became a teacher and philosopher. He traveled widely in ancient China looking for a ruler who would put into practice his Confucian teachings about goodness and humane government. However, during the Warring States period, few rulers were interested in goodness, because they were preoccupied with warfare and survival.

Mencius wrote a book about his teachings, which became one of the basic classics of Confucianism. He taught that if a ruler was bad, he would lose the Mandate of Heaven. The people would then have a right to rebel against him and follow a new ruler who would govern well.

THE EMPRESS WU

Throughout history, many Chinese empresses influenced their husbands and sons who occupied the Dragon Throne, but the Empress Wu was the only "female emperor" in Chinese history, the only woman who ruled the country in her own right.

She was born in A.D. 625, and became a

concubine in the palace of the second Tang emperor at the age of thirteen. Later she was sent to a Buddhist convent, but then was brought back to the palace. She became empress in 655 and took control of the government when her husband became ill for the last twenty-three years of his life. She ruthlessly eliminated her rivals, and gained the support of key military officials.

In 690, at the age of sixty-five, she proclaimed herself empress when her husband died. Many Confucian officials opposed her because they felt that it was wrong for a woman to rule. She in turn favored Buddhism over Confucianism. Empress Wu was capable of great cruelty and ruthlessness, but she governed efficiently and well. Under her rule, the Tang dynasty was peaceful, wealthy, and culturally brilliant.

Empress Wu retired in 705, and was succeeded by her son.

LI BO AND DU FU

Li Bo (701-762) and Du Fu (712-770) are widely regarded as the two greatest poets in Chinese history. Although they lived at the same time and were acquainted with each other, they were very different in their personalities, their careers, and their writing styles.

Li Bo studied Daoism as a young man. He married, but was unable to settle down. He preferred a life devoted to drinking, traveling around the empire, and writing poetry celebrating the pleasures of life. Eventually his poems brought him to the attention of the imperial court, and he was invited to the capital to join a group of poets supported by the emperor. He often got into trouble for drinking and fighting, but he was always forgiven because the emperor liked his poetry so much. Eventually he left the capital to become a wanderer, and died while traveling in eastern China.

Du Fu was born into a well-to-do family and given a classical Confucian education. He failed the imperial examinations, however, and so did not qualify for a government position. He became a teacher, and amused himself by traveling and writing poetry. During his travels he met Li Bo, and they later corresponded but did not meet again.

His poetry eventually won him a position at court. In 753 the empire was shaken when a general named An Lushan rebelled, and the emperor went into exile in Sichuan Province for several years. Du Fu accompanied the emperor to Sichuan, and eventually settled there, living in a small thatched house in conditions of hardship and poverty. His poems criticized the luxury and extravagance of the imperial court, and showed sympathy for the sufferings of ordinary people.

ZHU XI

During the late Tang and early Song dynasties, Buddhism declined in China while there was a great revival of interest in Confucianism. The Confucian revival was the work of many great scholars and philosophers, but the greatest Confucian thinker of the age was Zhu Xi (1130-1200). He wrote many books explaining the teachings of Confucius and his disciples, and his interpretations became the basis for later Chinese understanding of Confucianism. Zhu Xi is sometimes called "the Thomas Aquinas of China."

MARCO POLO

Marco Polo (1254-1324) was born in Venice. His father and uncle had once traveled to China along the Silk Route, and when Marco was old enough, they took him along on a return trip. He spent twenty-five years traveling in Asia, including about seventeen years at the court of the Mongol emperor of China, Kublai Khan. When he returned to Europe, he got into trouble in Genoa and was thrown into prison. There, he told tales of his adventures in China to a fellow prisoner, who wrote them down. The Book of Marco Polo contains many exaggerations, but it also gives a great deal of information about life in China during the Yuan dynasty. The book became an instant success in Europe, and was translated into many languages. It was partly responsible for inspiring other European explorers to travel in search of the riches of China.

Index

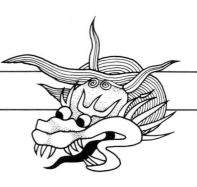

abacus 28, 42
acupuncture 20, 42
agriculture 12, 14
ancestors 18
ancestor worship 23
animals 12
archery 35
architecture 10, 33
arms and armor 37
art 32, 33
astrologers 25
astrology 28, 42
astronomy 28, 39
Amur River 11

bamboo 12, 33, 40
battles 37
Beijing 33, 34
birds 12
block printing 28, 40
boats 34
bodhisattva 25, 42
books 27, 40
bound feet 22
Bo Zhuyi 29
bronze 32, 39
Buddha 24, 35, 42
Buddhism 10, 20, 24, 25, 31, 35, 44, 45
building bricks 16, 33

calendar 28, 35, 39
calligraphy 32, 33, 35, 42
canals 11, 34, 39
carp 12, 15, 42
cavalry 37
censors 26, 42
ceremonies 25
children 18
chopsticks 19, 42
civilization, decline of 41
civil wars 37
climate 11

clothes 18, 21, 22
colors 22
communication 34
compass 40
concubines 18, 42
Confucianism 23, 24, 45
Confucius 10, 23, 26, 29, 35, 44
cosmetics 22
counting rods 28
courtyards 16, 33, 35
crops 12, 14, 15
crossbow 37

dance 35
Daoism 10, 20, 24, 31, 35, 42, 44
delta 11, 42
Diamond Sutra 27
diet 19
divination 27, 42
doctors 20
domestic animals 15
dowry 25
dragons 30
drawloom 33, 42
Du Fu 29, 45
dynasty 6–7, 9–10, 42

earthquakes 33
education 18, 35, 40
embroidery 21
emperor 9, 17, 26, 41, 42
Empress Wu 44, 45
entertainers 35
Europeans 10, 38, 41
examination system 26, 29, 43
exploration 34

families 17
farmers 11, 16, 18
feasts 19

festivals 35, 36
feudalism 43
fireworks 36, 40
fishing 15
food 19
Forbidden City 33, 44
funerals 19, 22, 25

games 35
gardens 16, 33
ginseng 20, 43
gods 24, 30
government 26
Grand Canal 10, 34
Great Wall of China 9
gunpowder 38, 40

hairstyles 21, 22
Han dynasty 6, 10, 23, 24, 26, 31, 33, 37, 39, 40
hats 21
health 19
hemp 21, 43
herbal remedies 20, 43
Himalayas 11
houses 16, 17
Huang He River see Yellow River
hunting 15

ibex 13
ideograms 27
imperial dress 21
imperial symbols 21
inventions 40
iron 39
irrigation 11, 14

jade 32, 43
junks 34, 43

kang 17
karma 24, 43

kites   35
Kong Fuzi *see* Confucius
kowtowing   25, 43
Kublai Khan   39, 45

lacquer   33
landforms   11
Laozi   44
law   26
Legalism   10, 26
legends and literature   29, 30, 31
Li Bo   29, 45
loess   11, 14, 43
Longmen caves   44

magicians   25
magistrate   16, 26, 43
mah-jong   35
Manchus   10, 21
Mandarin   43
mandate of heaven   10, 43, 44
mangrove swamps   12
marriage   17, 18, 25
measures   28
medical encyclopedias   20
medicine   19, 20
men   17–18
Mencius   44
men's clothes   21
metalworking   39
Middle Kingdom   9, 26
military examinations   38
millet   14, 43
Ming dynasty   7, 10, 32, 34, 41, 44
Mongols   10, 37
monsoons   11
months   28
moveable type   27–28, 40
moxibustion   20, 43
mulberry   12, 15, 27, 39
music   35
musical instruments   35
mythology   30, 31

names   17
New Year   36
nirvana   24, 43
numbers   28

officers   37
opium   41

paddy fields   14, 43
pagoda   43
painting   32, 33, 35
palaces   33
pandas   13
pantomime   35
paper   27, 32, 40
phoenix   30
plants   12
plays   35
plows   14
poetry   29, 35, 45
Polo, Marco   9, 10, 45
porcelain   10, 32, 34, 39, 41
pottery   32, 39
printing   27, 40

qilin   30
Qin dynasty   6, 9, 10, 26, 28, 37, 41
Qing dynasty   7, 10, 20, 21, 41, 44

ramie   15, 21, 43
rebellions   37, 41
recreation   35
reincarnation   43
religion   23, 24, 25
rice   14, 17, 19
rituals   25, 35
roads   34, 39

sampans   34, 43
scrolls   27, 40
servants   18
Shang dynasty   7, 10, 27, 32, 37, 41
Siddhartha Gautama *see* Buddha
silk   18, 21, 32, 33, 34, 39, 41
Silk Route   9, 34, 39, 43, 45
silkworms   15, 18, 39
Song dynasty   6, 10, 20, 22, 28, 31, 32, 33, 39, 40, 44
Sui dynasty   7, 10, 34
sundials   28

Tang dynasty   7, 10, 20, 29, 31, 32, 39, 40
tea   19
temples   23, 33, 35
textiles   33
theater   35
Tibet   11
time   28
trade   16, 34
transportation   34

war   37
Warring States period   10
waterways   34
weaving   33
Wei dynasty   44
weights   28
wheat   11
women   18
women's clothes   22
writing   27

Xia dynasty   10

yamen   16, 43
Yangtse River   11
Yellow River   10, 11
yin and yang   20, 43
Yuan dynasty   6, 10, 28, 44
Yun'gang caves   44

Zhou dynasty   7, 10, 21, 29, 32, 34, 37, 39, 41, 44
Zhu Xi   45